Space Scientist
THE
STARS

Heather Couper

Franklin Watts

London   New York   Toronto   Sydney

© 1985 Franklin Watts
Limited

First published in 1985 by
Franklin Watts Limited
12a Golden Square
London W1R 4BA

First published in the USA
by Franklin Watts Inc.
387 Park Avenue South
New York, N.Y. 10016

First published in Australia
by Franklin Watts
Australia
1 Campbell Street
Artarmon, NSW 2064

UK ISBN: 0 86313 268 5
US ISBN: 0-531-10054-5
Library of Congress
Catalog Card No:
85-51134

Illustrations by
Drawing Attention
Rob Burns
Eagle Artists
Ron Jobson
Michael Roffe

Photographs supplied by
Nigel Henbest

Designed by
David Jefferis

Printed in Italy

Space Scientist

THE
STARS

Contents

The starry sky

On a dark, clear night, away from city lights, the sky can seem ablaze with stars. It's a sight many city-dwellers don't see very often – and then it looks as if there are millions of stars up there. In fact, even on the clearest night, you can see about 3,000 stars at most. And although they look like tiny dots, every star is a powerful, brilliant sun in its own right. The stars only appear small and faint because they're so far away.

People in the past depended on the stars much more than we do today. In the days before accurate clocks, astronomers used them to tell the time, watching as certain stars rose and set. Farmers noticed that different stars came round with each changing season and used them as signals to know when to plant or harvest their crops. And nearly 2,000 years ago sailors used the stars to navigate by. Noticing

that they saw different stars as they traveled long distances north or south of their home port, they were able to work out that the world was not flat, but round instead.

To tell one star from another, our ancestors grouped them together into imaginary patterns called constellations. Every different civilization had its own constellation patterns. For instance, while the Greeks imagined one pattern as looking like a queen sitting in a chair, the ancient Chinese astronomers divided it up into a rider with a team of horses and a path across the mountains! People learned to remember the constellation patterns by legends and folk stories which were woven around the characters they represented. The star maps on pages 28–9 show the constellations we use today. Learning to identify the patterns is the first step in getting to know the stars.

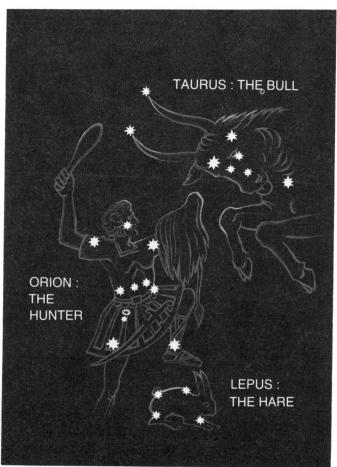

TAURUS : THE BULL

ORION :
THE
HUNTER

LEPUS :
THE HARE

◁ Ancient Greek astronomers imagined Orion, the Hunter, standing on a hare while driving away Taurus, the Bull.

△ Away from city lights and pollution, star patterns look brilliant. This is a view looking south early on a winter's evening when Orion is in the sky.

SKY TRAILS

The stars rise and set because the Earth spins around once every day. But one star – the Pole Star – stays almost still. That's because Earth's North Pole points toward it, so we appear to turn beneath it. If you have a camera with a "B" setting, aim it at the Pole Star and keep the shutter open for over half an hour. The "star trails" on your photograph show that the Earth is spinning.

How far are the stars?

Because the stars never move out of their constellation patterns – unlike the Sun, Moon and planets, which wander against the starry background – astronomers began to realize that the stars must be much further away. But the stars are so remote that no one succeeded in measuring the distance to one until 1838. That year Frederick Bessel found that 61 Cygni – a faint star in the constellation of Cygnus, the Swan – lay 100 trillion kilometers away!

Bessel used a method called parallax to find 61 Cygni's distance. This involves measuring the tiny shift in a nearby star's position against a background of distant stars when it is viewed from opposite sides of our path around the Sun. The nearer the star, the bigger the parallax shift will be – and then it's a simple matter of geometry to calculate its distance. But it's not at all simple to measure the tiny shift.

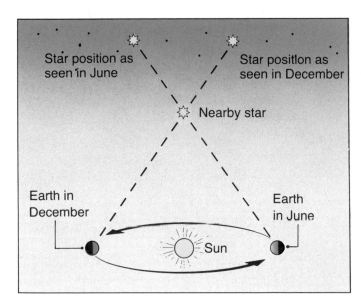

△ Astronomers use parallax to measure the distance to the nearest stars. A nearby star will appear to "wobble" to and fro when viewed from opposite sides of Earth's orbit.

The shift for the nearest star corresponds to the diameter of a penny seen over 2 km (1.2 miles) away!

The nearest star after the Sun is faint red Proxima Centauri, one of three stars making up the Alpha Centauri system (visible only from the southern hemisphere). But even Proxima lies 40 trillion kilometers away! To cope with such enormous numbers, astronomers have invented a "shorthand" to make them more manageable. Instead of using kilometers, they express distances to stars in terms of the time it takes their light to reach us. The speed of light is a very fundamental quantity because, at 300,000 km/s, it's the speed limit of the Universe. Since light from Proxima takes 4.3 years to reach us, we say that Proxima is 4.3 light years away. The enormous speed of light means that a light year is a vast distance – about 9.5 trillion kilometers!

Other stars are much more remote than Proxima. Sirius, the brilliant "Dog Star," is 8.7 light years away; red Betelgeuse in Orion lies at 650 light years; while southern hemisphere Canopus is 1,170 light years away.

ROAD TO THE STARS

It's impossible to get any real feel for the distances to the stars, especially when they're expressed in light years. But you can get some idea by imagining a journey to the nearest star by Earth-based transport. Proxima is 40 trillion km away.

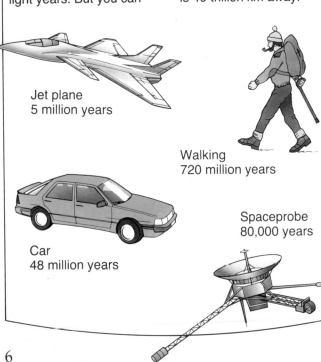

Jet plane
5 million years

Walking
720 million years

Car
48 million years

Spaceprobe
80,000 years

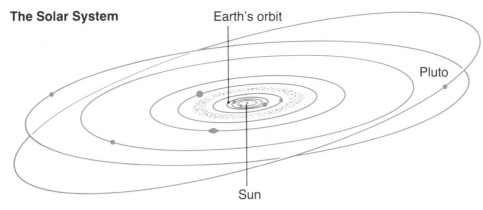

The Solar System

Earth's orbit

Pluto

Sun

◁ The Solar System is tiny and unimportant on the scale of the Universe. Although Pluto, the furthest planet, lies 6 billion km from the Sun, even the *nearest* star is 6,000 times further away. There are over 100,000 million stars in our wheel-shaped Milky Way Galaxy, which measures 100,000 light years across.

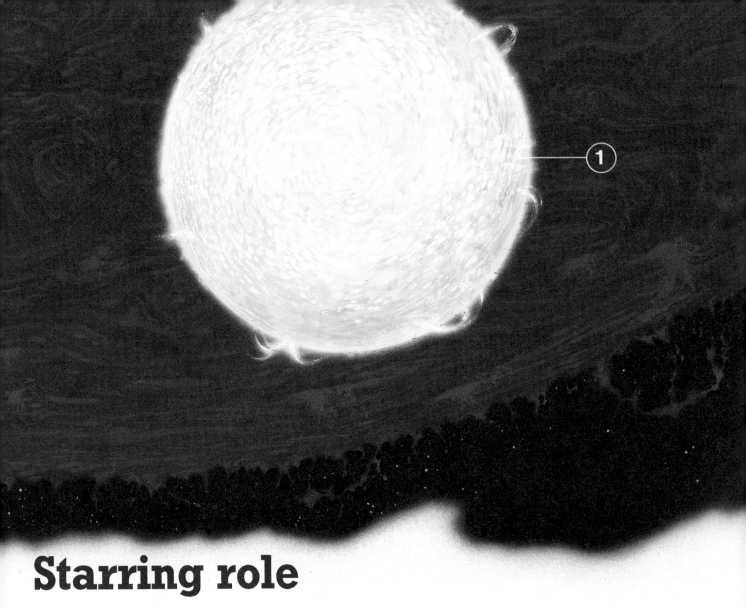

Starring role

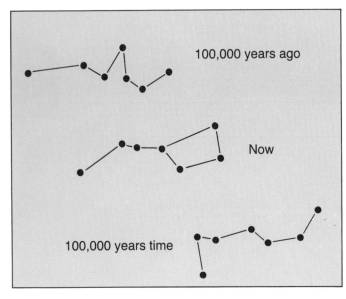

△ Seen over a period of thousands of years, the familiar shape of today's Big Dipper changes as the stars move through space. The middle five stars move together as a loose group.

100,000 years ago

Now

100,000 years time

Once astronomers have measured the distance to a star, they are able to find out all sorts of other things about it – its speed through space, how bright it is, and even how big or how heavy it is.

All the stars are moving through space. They circle the center of our Galaxy, just as the planets orbit the Sun. But because the stars are so far away, their movement in a human lifetime is far too small to be detected except by sensitive instruments.

But even a glance at the stars reveals that they have different brightnesses. The brightness we register on Earth is only a star's *apparent* brightness, however. Some stars look brilliant, like Alpha Centauri, but that's only because they are nearby. Others, like the Pole Star, appear fainter because they're so distant.

The brightness a star appears to have in the

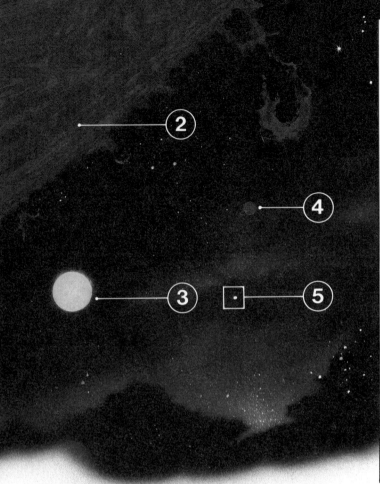

Types of stars		
Blue-white	25,000°C	
White	10,000°C	
Yellow	5,000°C	
Orange	4,000°C	
Red	3,000°C	
Color	**Surface temperature**	

△ Although the stars range widely in size, mass and brightness, our Sun is an average star. It's shown here with stars which are extreme:

1 Spica, 1,500 times brighter than the Sun.
2 Antares, a red giant.
3 The Sun.
4 Proxima, dim and red.
5 Sirius B, a white dwarf.

△ The color of a star is a guide to its temperature. The hottest stars of all, like Rigel or Spica, are blue-white. White stars like Sirius come next, followed by yellow stars like the Sun. Cooler still are orange stars such as Arcturus, while red stars like Betelgeuse are the coolest of all.

sky is called its apparent magnitude, and for most "naked-eye" stars the magnitude scale runs from 1 to 6. First-magnitude stars, like Rigel or Deneb, appear brightest. They're $2\frac{1}{2}$ times brighter than stars of magnitude 2, which in turn are $2\frac{1}{2}$ times brighter than stars of magnitude 3. The dimmest stars visible to the unaided eye are magnitude 6 – 100 times fainter than first-magnitude stars. The magnitudes themselves are subdivided for accuracy, so that the Pole Star, for example, has a magnitude of 2.1. The brightest stars of all are assigned zero or even negative magnitudes – which is why Sirius measures *minus* 1.44. When you know a star's magnitude and its actual distance, you can find out how luminous it *really* is.

Stars also cover quite a wide temperature span, and this is revealed in a star's color.

Although most stars appear white, a good look – particularly through binoculars – will show their subtle colors. Just as a metal bar heated in a fire will first glow red, then amber, followed by yellow, white and finally blue-white, so the stars' colors range from dull red to searing blue.

In all respects, the range among the stars is tremendous. There are single stars, double stars, multiple stars, stars thousands of times brighter than the Sun and thousands of times fainter, tiny stars the size of planets and huge ones as big as the diameter of Jupiter's orbit. Some stars even vary erratically in size and brightness.

Nearly all the "extremes" are phases every star passes through during its life. To see how the different stages fit in, we need to follow the life story of a star.

Starbirth

Although it may look like one at first, the middle "star" in Orion's sword (*see* picture on page 5) is not a star at all. Take a close look at it on a really clear night – better still, through a pair of binoculars – and you'll see that it's actually a glowing patch of gas, known to astronomers as a nebula. Like the hundreds of other nebulae in our Galaxy, the Orion Nebula is a huge gas cloud in which stars have just been born. The energetic radiation from the young stars embedded within excites the nebula to glow.

Starbirth begins when the gas and dust scattered between the stars becomes clumped together into huge dark clouds. Deep within, where it's undisturbed, the gas cloud starts to collapse under the pull of its own gravity. After a while the middle of the cloud breaks up into smaller clumps, and each of these continues to shrink on its own. As time goes by, each clump grows hotter as its gas becomes more and more compressed. Eventually each becomes so hot that it switches on its own source of nuclear energy. The clumps are now stars, generating their own light and heat.

For the first part of their lives, the young stars – clustered together like a clutch of eggs in a nest – are still surrounded by the glowing tatters of the gas cloud from which they were born. But their fierce radiation soon drives the nebula away, perhaps to form stars next time around.

Now the cluster shines unobscured, looking like jewels scattered against a velvet background. In time, though, even the cluster will break up as its stars begin to make their own way around the Galaxy. By this stage the young stars are fully grown up.

◁ The Orion Nebula, as it would appear from an imaginary planet lying nearby. The nebula is part of an enormous cloud of dust and gas, and it is excited to glow by a small cluster of stars called the Trapezium.

△ Mixed in with the gas in a nebula are particles of dust – "cosmic soot" from the surfaces of cool stars. But the dark Horsehead Nebula (also in Orion) will become bright as soon as stars begin to be born inside it.

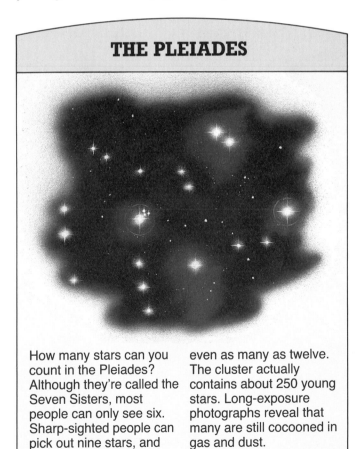

THE PLEIADES

How many stars can you count in the Pleiades? Although they're called the Seven Sisters, most people can only see six. Sharp-sighted people can pick out nine stars, and even as many as twelve. The cluster actually contains about 250 young stars. Long-exposure photographs reveal that many are still cocooned in gas and dust.

How stars work

By having the Sun, an average star, on our doorstep, astronomers can get a good idea of how *all* stars work. And one of the most powerful tools in unlocking the secrets of the stars is the prism (or today, the diffraction grating).

If you pass sunlight (or starlight) through a prism, it spreads out into a rainbow. The rainbow, which comes from hot gases below the Sun's surface, is crossed by patterns of dark lines from cooler gases near the surface itself. Each pattern is produced by a different chemical element, such as iron, sulfur, oxygen and so on. And so by looking at these spectral

lines, an astronomer can tell what the Sun – or any star – is made of. The Sun is made entirely of hot gas: three-quarters hydrogen, one-quarter helium, plus tiny amounts of the other elements. Most stars have a similar chemical make-up.

By knowing what conditions are like at the Sun's surface, astronomers can predict what kinds of things will happen deep in the Sun's core. There, the pressures and temperatures must be so high that the Sun's hydrogen gas is welded into helium, the next element up. This process of nuclear fusion keeps all the stars shining. Every time fusion takes place, a little bit of the Sun's mass is converted to energy – and it's this which eventually streams out as sunshine. But the Sun has so much matter that it converts 4 million tons of itself into energy every second!

Over thousands of years this energy works

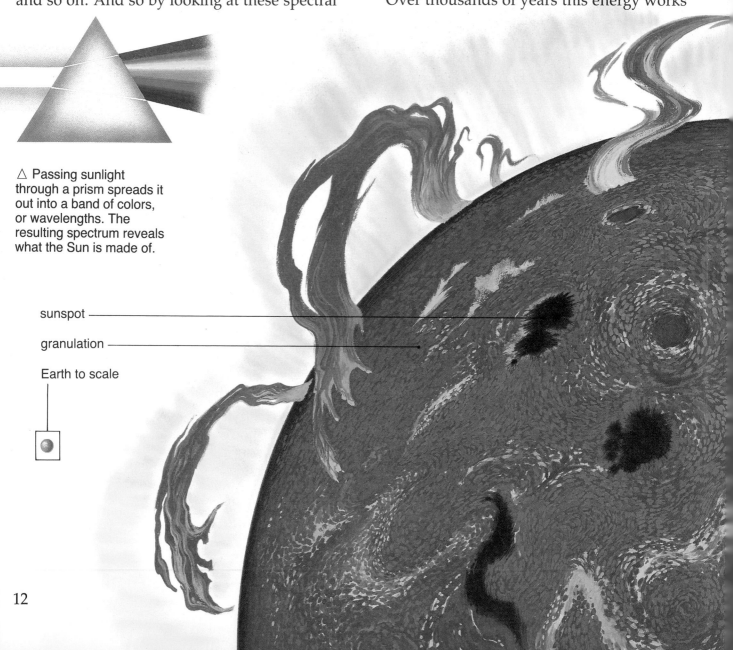

△ Passing sunlight through a prism spreads it out into a band of colors, or wavelengths. The resulting spectrum reveals what the Sun is made of.

sunspot

granulation

Earth to scale

its way to the Sun's surface, or photosphere, which seethes and bubbles like fat in a pan. In places the bubbling is disturbed by dark sunspots, where powerful magnetic fields hold back the gas currents. Above, in the Sun's atmosphere, these magnetic disturbances give rise to huge arches of glowing gas, or prominences, and even sudden explosions, or flares. Every eleven years or so the Sun becomes particularly active in this way. At "sunspot maximum" there are sometimes more than a dozen spot groups on the Sun's face at once. The resulting flares may be so powerful that they disrupt radio broadcasts on Earth, and their radiation can even be hazardous to manned spacecraft.

But the Sun is a very stable and dependable star. It has given us all our energy for the past 5 billion years – and it will continue to do so for 5 billion years to come.

SOLAR ECLIPSES

Total eclipse

Partial eclipse

Annular eclipse

To see the Sun's outer atmosphere, its corona, you must wait for a total eclipse of the Sun. Then the Moon completely blots out the Sun's brilliant disc. But you have to be in exactly the right spot on Earth to see the line-up, otherwise the eclipse is only partial. Annular eclipses take place when the Moon is too far from the Earth to cover the Sun.

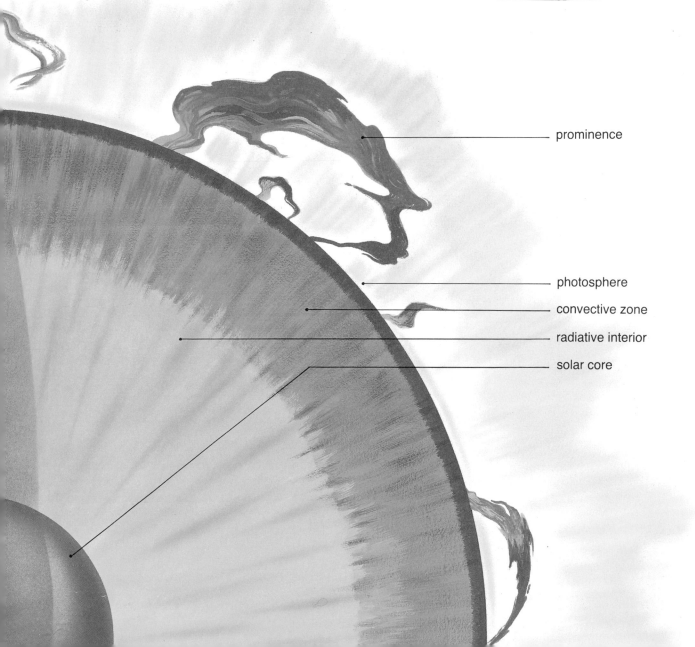

prominence

photosphere

convective zone

radiative interior

solar core

Double stars

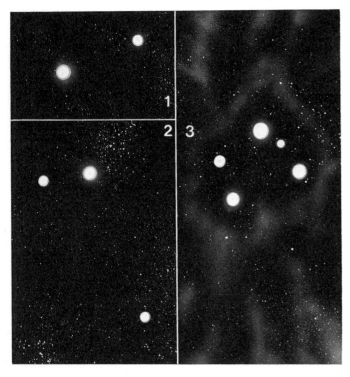

△ **1** 61 Cygni is a nearby pair of orange stars.
2 Sigma Orionis has blue and red companions.
3 Theta Orionis – the Trapezium – in Orion.

▷ Some stars are so close that they touch. Here a futuristic spaceprobe heads into the cocoon of gas stirred up by two stars' gravitational tug-of-war.

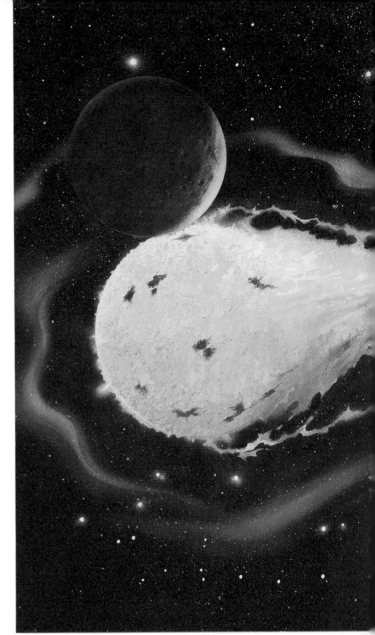

Our Sun is just a little unusual in being a star all on its own, because nearly 60 per cent of all stars come in pairs or even multiple groups. This isn't too surprising; it just means that two or three stars have managed to hold together from their early days as companions in a young star cluster.

Some stars in the sky are very obvious doubles. There's Mizar and its companion Alcor in the Big Dipper's handle for instance, although it's still not certain whether these stars are really associated or just seen in the same direction. But the two stars making up Epsilon Lyrae (close to Vega) most certainly do circle each other – and through a telescope you can see that each star is double again! Some double stars are so close that they pull off gas from one another.

Star pairs as close as this are called spectroscopic binaries, because you need a spectroscope – and not just a telescope – in order to distinguish them. The most famous binary of this kind is Algol, in Perseus. Its two stars are so close that they orbit one another in only 2½ days – and it just happens that the orbits are at such an angle to us that one star passes directly in front of the other during the period. Because one star is so much larger and dimmer than its hot, bright companion, the *total* brightness we see from the system falls by more than half when the dim star is in front.

Variable stars

Algol may look like a variable star, but it's just a special kind of double. However, there are many genuine variable stars, and many amateur astronomers measure their brightness every night. Some stars vary because they

swell and shrink. Among these are the huge
red giant stars (see pages 16–17), which vary in
an irregular way over periods of about a year.
Smaller stars can swell and shrink more
rapidly. Some of these pulsating stars, like the
brilliant Cepheids, have pulsation periods
closely tied to their actual brightness.
Astronomers can use stars like this as
"standard candles" to measure distances far
out in space, beyond the reach of parallax.

But the ultimate variable stars are the novae.
They aren't actually new stars, as their name
suggests, but shrunken, collapsed stars living
in double-star systems. If their companion
dumps material on them, they can flare up to
many thousands of times their previous
brightness before fading away again. Many
novae are discovered by amateur astronomers,
and one nova hunter has five to his credit!

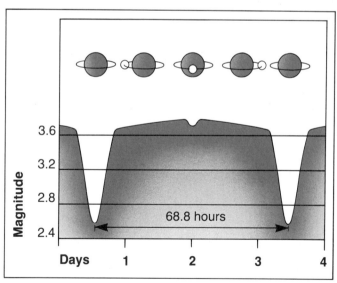

△ Although Algol's light
drops by half every 2½
days, it is not a variable
star. As the diagram
shows, a cool, dim
companion orbits the
smaller, brighter star and
periodically blocks off its
light. Algol is an eclipsing
binary star.

Star death

Eventually all stars must die. The end comes when they run out of fuel: when there is no longer enough hydrogen in the core to keep the star shining. Fortunately for us, our Sun – and all other average, low-mass stars – use up their fuel relatively slowly. This means that their lives are long. Our Sun, at 5,000 million years old, is middle-aged, but it still has another 5,000 million years to go.

When this time is up, the Sun's fuel supply will start to dwindle. As its energy-flow dries up, its core will start to collapse in on itself. Strangely enough, this will heat up the outer layers so that they billow out – but they will grow cooler and redder as they expand. The huge distended Sun will now become a red giant star, like Betelgeuse or Antares. It may swell up to more than 100 times its present size. And by this stage Mercury, Venus – and possibly the Earth – will have been engulfed by its encroaching surface.

It will be small comfort to life on Earth to know that the red giant phase is a brief one in a star's life. Red giants, rarefied and distended, are hopelessly unstable. Their outer layers

swell and shrink, making the whole star change in brightness. After just a few million years, a red giant gently puffs away its flimsy atmosphere, revealing its dense, collapsed core. For a few moments of cosmic time, the core lights up the dispersing atmosphere as a planetary nebula – and then that, too, is gone.

Left behind is the star's core – a bizarre object called a white dwarf. With the mass of a

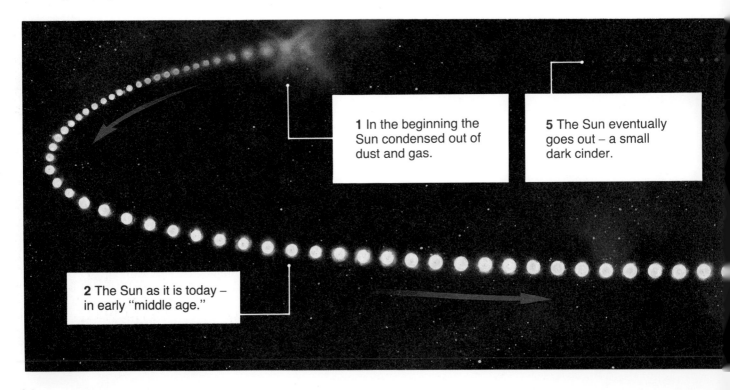

1 In the beginning the Sun condensed out of dust and gas.

5 The Sun eventually goes out – a small dark cinder.

2 The Sun as it is today – in early "middle age."

star, but shrunken to the size of a planet, this relic is so compressed that just one teaspoonful of its matter would weigh a ton! But its days are numbered, for it has no energy source. All it can do is leak away its heat into space, cooling from white through yellow, orange, red, dull red … In the end all stars like the Sun will become cold, black cinders, orbited by the forlorn remains of their dead planets.

△ Three planetary nebulae: the Ring (Lyra), the Dumbbell (Vulpecula) and the Helix (Aquarius). The gas shell is probably the cast-off atmosphere of an old red giant.

▽ Life story of a star like the Sun. A star's life and death are part of a cycle; material ejected from "dying" stars will be used to make new stars the next time around.

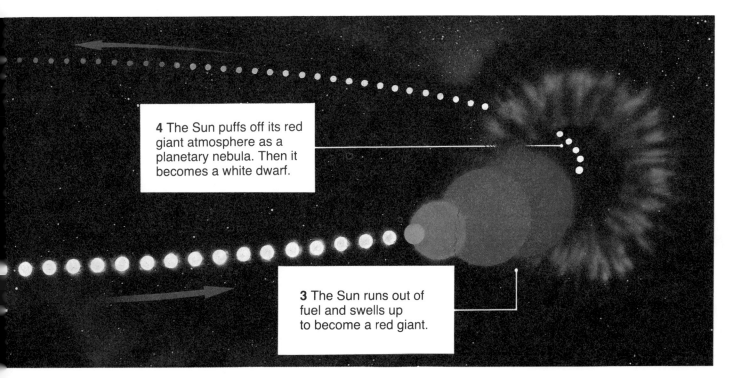

4 The Sun puffs off its red giant atmosphere as a planetary nebula. Then it becomes a white dwarf.

3 The Sun runs out of fuel and swells up to become a red giant.

Supernova!

◁ A supernova explosion is so powerful that, for a few weeks, the supernova can outshine its entire galaxy. No supernovae have been seen within our own Galaxy for nearly 400 years.

▷ The Crab Nebula is the remains of a supernova explosion seen by Chinese and Korean astronomers in AD 1054. The debris now covers a region 15 light years across.

Not all stars will die as quietly as "average" stars like the Sun. Really massive, brilliant stars, like Rigel in Orion and Deneb in Cygnus, rip through their nuclear fuel at an incredible rate. Because of their enormous mass, their central pressures and temperatures are considerably higher than in normal stars. This allows them to "fire" successively heavier and heavier gases to make energy. So when their cores run out of hydrogen, it's no problem: they can squeeze helium to make carbon, and carbon to make oxygen, and so on.

But there's a point beyond which even fusion cannot go. When the star tries to create energy out of a core made of iron, the core simply breaks up – in a matter of minutes. The net result is a full-scale star explosion, called a supernova. A supernova can outshine a whole galaxy of 1,000 million stars. But because the kinds of star which "go supernova" are uncommon, so too are supernovae; the last to be seen in our Galaxy was as long ago as 1604. Astronomers must be content to study those in other galaxies millions of light years away.

One of the most famous supernovae was the star seen to explode in AD 1054 by astronomers in China. The astronomers at the time had no idea they were witnessing the death of a star, but reported that the "guest star" appeared like "half a bamboo mat in the sky" and shone with "the five colors, both pleasing and otherwise." For several weeks the star was so bright that it could be seen during daylight. The explosion gave rise to the Crab Nebula, which telescopes reveal today as a mass of tangled filaments expanding at a rate of 4 million km/hr into space.

But supernovae are not all death and destruction. The demise of a star creates shockwaves in the thin sprinkling of gas and dust between the stars. This compresses the gas and can trigger the birth of new stars – and their surrounding planets. The new stars and their planets are enriched with chemicals which were first forged in the dead star's core. The carbon which makes up the rich variety of life we find on Earth was once part of the core of a star which exploded. Without supernovae, there would have been no life.

△ Like a string of wispy cirrus clouds in space, the Veil Nebula is just an arc of an enormous bubble caused by the explosion of a star 20,000 years ago.

As the bubble continues to expand, it compresses the gas ahead of it. Eventually, this will trigger the birth of new stars and planets – and perhaps living beings.

When a supernova explodes, it sometimes happens that not all of it is destroyed. Just as an average star leaves a white dwarf behind, sometimes a star corpse remains. But as we'll see on the following pages, some of these "corpses" seem to have lives of their own.

Pulsars

In the autumn of 1967 radio astronomers at Cambridge, using a new telescope for the first time, were baffled to pick up astonishingly regular, rapid pulses from the sky. Were the pulses artificial – generated by alien life? With tongue in cheek, the astronomers nicknamed the source of the pulses LGM-1 – "Little Green Man-1."

We now know that the pulses are completely natural, and LGM-1 (under its official title of CP 1919) has been joined by hundreds of similar objects: pulsars. Pulsars are thought to be the super-compressed cores remaining after a star explodes as a supernova, when the "relic" left is too massive to settle as a white dwarf. Pulsars are so compressed that the protons and electrons making up their atoms have been forced together to make neutrons.

The compression also "amplifies" the spin of these tiny stars. By the time one of them is the size of a typical city – about 25 km (15 miles) across – it spins around nearly once per second. The pulsar's super-concentrated magnetic field makes it generate flashes of radiation like the rotating beam of a lighthouse, giving rise to the pulses we detect on Earth. One of the most famous pulsars lies at the heart of the Crab Nebula, pulsing 30 times a second!

In time, pulsars lose energy by radiating, and the pulsar becomes a quiet, non-pulsing neutron star. But neutron stars are still ultra-compressed. Their gravitational pull is so strong that you would have to travel at half the speed of light to escape from one. If a neutron star has a close companion star, it can snatch and heat up its gases so fiercely that the system emits searing X rays. X-ray satellites have pinpointed the location of many neutron stars.

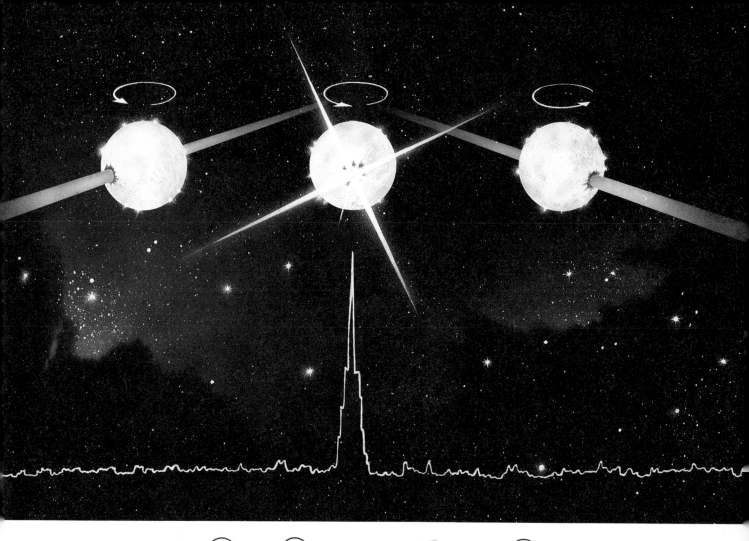

△ A pulsar has a "hot spot" on its surface. When the beam points toward us, radio telescopes pick up its "pulses."

▽ Next to a red giant star, the Sun seems very small. But the Sun is very much bigger than a planet-sized white dwarf – which in turn is thousands of times larger than an island-sized neutron star.

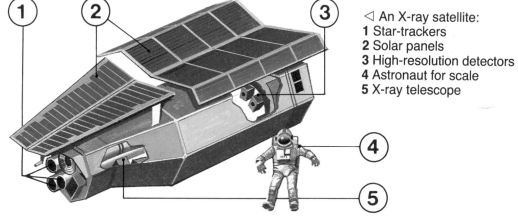

◁ An X-ray satellite:
1 Star-trackers
2 Solar panels
3 High-resolution detectors
4 Astronaut for scale
5 X-ray telescope

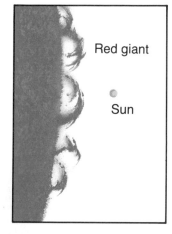

Red giant

Sun

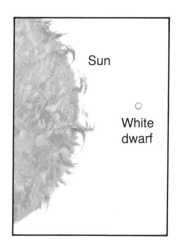

Sun

White dwarf

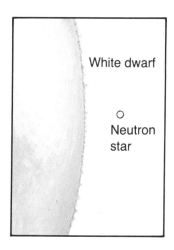

White dwarf

Neutron star

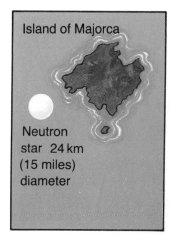

Island of Majorca

Neutron star 24 km (15 miles) diameter

Black holes

If a supernova leaves behind a core more than about three times more massive than the Sun, then not even the force exerted by neutrons can withstand the inpull of its gravity. The core suffers a runaway collapse. As it collapses, it reaches a stage at which the escape velocity

▽ Scientists regard black holes as distortions in the "material" of space into which things fall – like deep hollows in a rubber sheet.

from its surface approaches the speed of light. At this point no light can escape; and the object becomes black. It also forms a "hole" in space because, if anything falls "in," it can never escape again – nothing, as far as we know, can travel faster than light. And so the end result of a really massive star is a black hole.

Black holes are almost impossible to detect, and no one would claim for certain that any *have* been detected yet. But black holes with close companion stars offer a chance. We'd expect them to tear away their companion's gases, which would be heated fiercely enough to give out X rays before falling into the hole. X-ray satellites have pinpointed half a dozen "possible" black holes.

Although we can't see things falling into black holes, we can calculate what would happen if something did. In fact, even before

△ Seen from the surface of an imaginary planet, a black hole tears material away from the surface of a companion star in orbit about it.

The fiercely heated material forms a glaring accretion disc around the black hole before disappearing into the hole forever.

▽ The brightest star in this photograph, HDE 226868, may have a black hole in orbit about it. Astronomers have detected X rays coming from the star's dark companion. This mystery object appears to be about ten times more massive than the Sun – heavy enough to be a black hole.

falling in, an unfortunate victim would be distorted and elongated by the powerful gravitational forces – a process called "spaghettification"! A black hole seen close up would probably be surrounded by a whirling accretion disc of matter spiraling in rather like the scum around a drain. Once inside the black hole, there would be no escape. Scientists have worked out that anything falling into a black hole – whether it's the star that collapsed in the first place, an elephant, a spacecraft, or a mountain – would be compressed to an infinitesimally small point.

The only good news is that, despite sci-fi stories, you would have to be right on top of a black hole to be swallowed up! The gravity of a black hole, like that of everything else in the Universe, becomes weaker the further away you go.

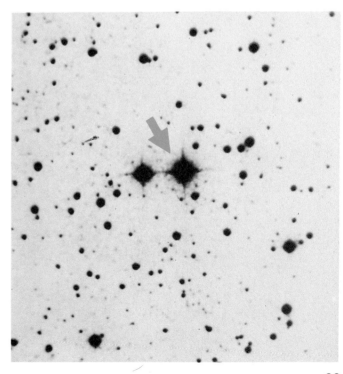

Some famous stars

The mystery of Sirius

Sirius is the brightest star in the sky. Its color is dazzling white. Sirius is also a double star, although its companion is hard to see. That's because it's a tiny white dwarf star, which – because Sirius is often called "The Dog Star" – goes by the nickname of "The Pup." But was "The Pup" once much brighter than Sirius, even in relatively recent times? And in particular, did some of our ancestors actually see "The Pup" at the end of its red giant phase? The puzzling thing is that some historical records, dating back to 2,000 years

△ Sirius is currently 10,000 times brighter than "The Pup," a white dwarf star. Some astronomers believe that people observing 2,000 years ago, who reported Sirius as "red," may have been seeing "The Pup" as a red giant. If true, "The Pup" would have been even brighter than Sirius today.

▽ The Three Wise Men who followed the Christmas Star to Bethlehem may not have been following a star at all, according to the latest calculations. It now seems possible that the "star" could instead have been three very close groupings of the two planets Jupiter and Saturn.

ago, describe the color of Sirius as definitely red. Sirius itself can never have been red – but there's just a chance that "The Pup" could have been.

Eta Carinae – lull before the storm

In the middle of the nineteenth century the southern hemisphere star Eta Carinae was the second brightest in the sky after Sirius. Since then it has faded so much that it is hardly visible to the unaided eye. But has Eta Carinae really faded? The star is shrouded in dense nebulosity, and it appears that Eta Carinae is only being dimmed because it is wreathed in a particularly thick dust cloud. The latest measurements show the star to be among the most luminous known, and its lifetime will be correspondingly short. One day it may emerge from its obscurity as a glaring supernova.

The Christmas Star

What was the Christmas Star, and did it really exist? If we search for evidence of astronomical events close to Jesus' birth (now dated by calendar experts at 7 BC), we find very little to go on.

For instance, there's no debris from novae or supernovae dating from that time; and no good evidence for any bright comets. In fact it looks now as if the "star" was not a star at all, but a pair of planets instead! Three times during 7 BC, Jupiter (King of the planets) and Saturn (Planet of the Jewish people) drew close enough together in the sky to appear as one. The two together would have appeared dazzling. Both planets were astrologically important to the Jewish people and they may have taken this as a sign that the King of the Jews would soon be born.

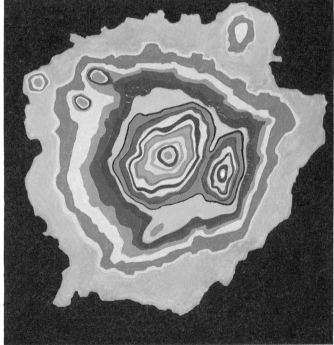

△ This peculiar "tapestry" is a computerized plot of the light from Eta Carinae, which makes it possible to peer through the murk surrounding the star. Eta Carinae itself is at the center, in the most densely contoured part. Surrounding it is a shell of material ejected by the star. The "eyes" at the top are other stars lying close by.

Seeing stars

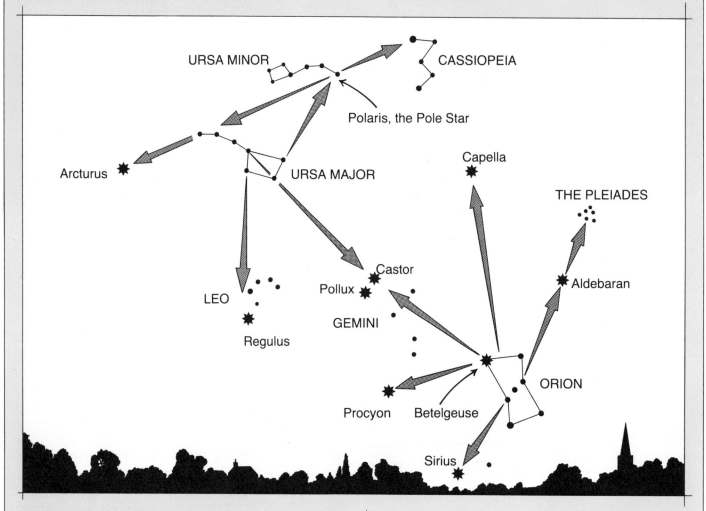

URSA MINOR

CASSIOPEIA

Polaris, the Pole Star

Arcturus

URSA MAJOR

Capella

THE PLEIADES

Aldebaran

Castor

Pollux

LEO

GEMINI

Regulus

ORION

Procyon   Betelgeuse

Sirius

You don't need a telescope to observe the stars. When you first start, a telescope is a positive drawback, because you need the widest possible view of the sky to learn the constellation patterns!

Binoculars show stars ten times fainter than your eyes can, although you see a smaller region of the sky. Buy those with the biggest lenses you can afford, and support them well – or they'll wobble! You can get marvelous views of the Milky Way and many nebulae.

Move on to a telescope when you're really ready, and be prepared for a shock – the views you get won't be like the long-exposure photographs in books. But there'll be enough up there to keep you busy for years, including clusters, nebulae, double and variable stars.

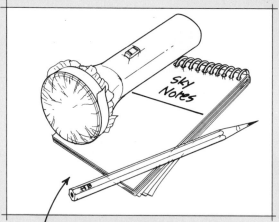

THIS BASIC KIT IS ALL YOU NEED FOR SUCCESSFUL SKYWATCHING. CHECK OPPOSITE FOR PLANISPHERE AND CLOTHES.

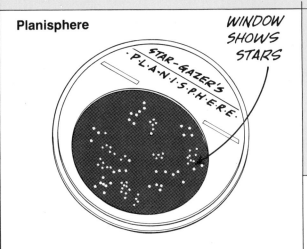

Planisphere

WINDOW SHOWS STARS

STAR-GAZER'S ·P·L·A·N·I·S·P·H·E·R·E·

△ A planisphere, or star-dial, is an ideal way to learn the constellations and find out when they're visible. You can "dial the sky" for any hour of the year. Make sure you buy a planisphere for your correct latitude!

▽ When you go out to observe, even in the height of summer, wrap up really well. Thick-soled boots are essential – you'll never enjoy the stars if you have cold feet! Wear lots of layers to trap the air next to your body, and invest in a pair of fingerless gloves. They're surprisingly warm and still let you use your fingers. Finally, don't forget a warm hat; one-fifth of your body heat escapes through the top of your head!

Clothing

Top ten skysights

Naked eye
Pleiades Beautiful cluster of stars.
Andromeda galaxy Galaxy of stars even bigger than the Milky Way.
Orion Brilliant, spectacular constellation.
The Milky Way Edge-on view of our own Galaxy.
Mizar and Alcor Double star in the Big Dipper's "handle."
***The Magellanic Clouds** Two companion galaxies to our own.
***The Coal Sack** Dark dust cloud next to the Southern Cross.
Algol Eclipsing binary star in Perseus.
Delphinus Constellation like a diving dolphin.
Scorpius Huge starry Scorpion.

***S. hemisphere only**

Binoculars
Orion Nebula Glowing cloud of gas and dust.
M13 Globular cluster of stars in Hercules.
Milky Way Marvelous views here.
Double cluster in Perseus Pair of little star clusters close together.
Andromeda galaxy It's so large that it is better viewed through binoculars rather than a telescope.
***Omega Centauri** Enormous globular cluster.
Lagoon Nebula Glowing gas cloud nearly twice as big as the Full Moon in extent. In Sagittarius.
Mira Ceti Variable red giant star.
Praesepe Star cluster in Cancer, sometimes called "The Beehive."
***The Jewel Box** Beautiful small cluster.

Telescope
Albireo Lovely yellow star with a blue companion, marking the "head" of Cygnus the Swan.
Orion Nebula Spectacular in any telescope.
M35 Pretty, star-shaped cluster of stars in Gemini.
Virgo cluster Cluster of several faint galaxies.
Epsilon Boötis Double star in Boötes.
Crab Nebula Remains of the supernova seen to explode in Taurus in 1054.
Ring Nebula Planetary nebula which looks like a tiny smoke-ring.
Whirlpool galaxy Faint spiral galaxy, linked by an arm to its companion.
Epsion Lyrae Famous double-double star.
Gamma Leonis Golden yellow star with a similar companion.

Star maps

JULY

AUGUST

JUNE

SEPTEMBER

MAY

OCTOBER

APRIL

NOVEMBER

MARCH

DECEMBER

FEBRUARY

JANUARY

Stars of northern skies

1 Andromeda	10 Capricornus	21 Gemini	32 Pisces
2 Aquarius	11 Cassiopeia	22 Hercules	33 Pisces Austrinus
3 Aquila	12 Centaurus	23 Hydra	34 Sagittarius
4 Aries	13 Cepheus	24 Leo	35 Scorpius
5 Auriga	14 Cetus	25 Lepus	36 Serpens Caput
6 Boötes	15 Columba	26 Libra	37 Serpens Cauda
7 Cancer	16 Corona Borealis	27 Lyra	38 Taurus
8 Canis Major	17 Corvus	28 Ophiucus	39 Ursa Major
9 Canis Minor	18 Cygnus	29 Orion	40 Ursa Minor
	19 Draco	30 Pegasus	41 Virgo
	20 Eridanus	31 Perseus	42 Milky Way

28

USE THE MAPS LIKE THIS – TURN THE BOOK UNTIL THE PRESENT MONTH IS AT THE BOTTOM. YOU SHOULD BE ABLE TO SEE THE STARS IN THE MIDDLE AND UPPER PART OF THE MAP.

THIS MAP SHOWS THE STARS VISIBLE FROM THE SOUTHERN HALF OF THE WORLD.

AUGUST
JULY
SEPTEMBER
JUNE
OCTOBER
MAY
NOVEMBER
APRIL
DECEMBER
MARCH
JANUARY
FEBRUARY

Stars of southern skies

1 Ara
2 Aries
3 Aquarius
4 Aquila
5 Cancer
6 Canis Major
7 Canis Minor
8 Capricornus
9 Carina
10 Centaurus

11 Cetus
12 Corona Borealis
13 Corvus
14 Crater
15 Crux
16 Cygnus
17 Delphinus
18 Eridanus
19 Gemini
20 Grus
21 Hercules
22 Hydra

23 Leo
24 Libra
25 Lupus
26 Monoceros
27 Octans
28 Ophiucus
29 Orion
30 Pegasus
31 Phoenix
32 Pisces
33 Pisces Austrinus
34 Sagitta

35 Sagittarius
36 Sculptor
37 Scorpius
38 Serpens
39 Taurus
40 Triangulum
41 Triangulum Australe
42 Vela
43 Virgo
44 Magellanic Clouds
45 Milky Way

29

Glossary

Accretion disc Disc of fiercely hot glowing matter spiraling into a black hole.

Atom The smallest part of an element – such as hydrogen, oxygen or carbon – which can take part in a chemical reaction.

Binary system A system of two stars in orbit about each other.

Black hole A collapsed object whose gravitational pull is so strong that nothing – not even light – can escape from its surface. Consequently, the object is black; and it's a hole because things which fall "in" can never escape.

Cepheid stars Very luminous white or yellow-white variable stars whose periods of variability are linked to their actual brightnesses. Astronomers use Cepheid stars to measure distances in space.

Constellation An imaginary grouping of stars in the sky, usually with a mythological name like Leo or Orion. Stars in a constellation are usually not associated, but spread out through space.

Dust Microscopic grains in space which absorb starlight. The grains themselves are probably "soot" from cool stars, and they sometimes clump together in huge dark clouds.

Eclipsing binary A double star placed at such an angle to us that the two stars pass periodically behind and in front of each other.

Electron Part of an atom. It's a tiny particle with a negative charge which circles the atom's nucleus like a planet circling the Sun.

Galaxy An "island" made of millions of stars. There are millions of galaxies in the Universe, separated by empty space. Our own Galaxy is written with a capital "G."

Gravity The force of attraction which is felt between two bodies, such as the stars in a binary system.

Light year The distance traveled by a ray of light in a year, 9.5 trillion kilometers.

Magnitude The brightness of a star, expressed on a scale of numbers. Bright stars have magnitudes in low numbers, dim stars in high numbers.

Mass The amount of matter making up a body. On Earth, mass is the same as weight.

Nebula A cloud of gas and dust in space.

Neutron An electrically neutral particle which forms part of the nucleus of an atom.

Neutron star A collapsed star composed mainly of neutrons. Pulsars are young, fast-spinning neutron stars.

Nova White dwarf star in a binary system which flares up thousands of times in brightness when its companion dumps matter on it.

Nuclear fusion Nuclear reaction in which hydrogen, under extreme heat and pressure, turns to helium. The energy which fusion releases keeps the stars shining.

Orbit The path followed by a planet, satellite or star in space.

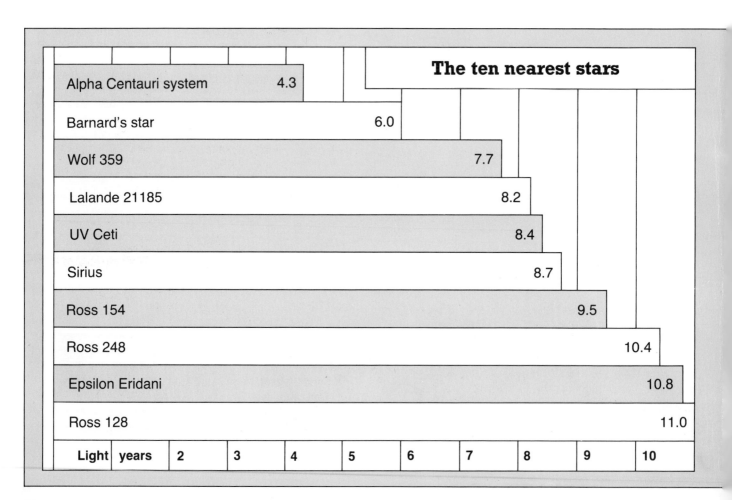

The ten nearest stars

	Light years								
Alpha Centauri system	4.3								
Barnard's star	6.0								
Wolf 359	7.7								
Lalande 21185	8.2								
UV Ceti	8.4								
Sirius	8.7								
Ross 154	9.5								
Ross 248	10.4								
Epsilon Eridani	10.8								
Ross 128	11.0								
	2	3	4	5	6	7	8	9	10

Parallax Shift in a nearby object's position when seen from two different vantage points. Astronomers use it to find the distance to nearby stars.

Photosphere The visible surface of the Sun or a star.

Planet Dark, low-mass body in orbit about a star.

Planetary nebula The shell of gas puffed off by an aging star before it becomes a white dwarf.

Pole star Polaris, the star which appears to be almost directly above Earth's North Pole. The Earth spins "under" it, and so it seems to stay still in the sky.

Proton A positively charged particle which forms part of the nucleus of an atom.

Radio telescope Telescope designed to pick up radio waves from objects in space.

Red giant Star near the end of its life, whose outer layers have billowed out and cooled down.

Spectrum The rainbow of colors which make up so-called "white" light. Each color – like the separate notes of a piano – corresponds to a different wavelength of radiation. The spectrum of a star reveals its chemical make-up.

Star A hot, massive, glowing body which generates energy through nuclear fusion reactions.

Supernova A massive star which explodes at the end of its life.

Variable star A star which varies in brightness. Many variable stars pulsate in and out.

White dwarf The collapsed core of a star like the Sun; all that is left after the dying star has blown off its outer layers as a planetary nebula.

The ten brightest stars

Star	Distance in light years	Magnitude
Sirius	8.7	−1.45
Canopus	1170	−0.73
Alpha Centauri	4.3	−0.10
Arcturus	36	−0.06
Vega	26	+0.04
Capella	45	+0.08
Rigel	900	+0.11
Procyon	11.5	+0.35
Achernar	120	+0.48
Beta Centauri	390	+0.60

Where to go, what to do

The United States is a world leader in astronomy, and there are lots of places you can visit to get an idea of how astronomers work. But one of the best ways to get really involved in astronomy is to join a local or national astronomical society.

Find out if there is a club in your home town by writing to The Astronomical League, c/o Tom J. Martinez, Editor, *The Reflector*, 1208 Somerset Court, Blue Springs, Missouri 64015. *The Reflector* keeps you up-to-date with news of local society events. In Canada the main astronomical association is the Royal Astronomical Society of Canada, 136 Dupont Street, Toronto, Ontario, Canada M5R 1VZ. This society is aimed at people who have some knowledge of astronomy, so you might feel happier joining a local club at first.

Once you've joined, you'll find plenty to do – like making new friends, going to meetings, having star parties, constructing telescopes, or visiting places of astronomical interest.

One of the best places to get to know the stars – apart from the night sky itself – is under the artificial "sky" of one of the many planetariums in the US and Canada. Here's a brief list of just a few of the major planetariums:
Adler Planetarium, Chicago, Illinois.
American Museum – Hayden Planetarium, New York, New York.
Griffith Observatory and Planetarium, Los Angeles, California.
Hansen Planetarium, Salt Lake City, Utah.
McLaughlin Planetarium, Toronto, Ontario.
H.R. Macmillan Planetarium, Vancouver, British Columbia.

As well as planetariums, the US and Canada have science centers where you can learn about astronomy through hands-on exhibits:
Ontario Science Center, Toronto, Ontario.
The Pacific Science Center, Seattle, Washington.

Many of the leading observatories in the United States have special Visitor Centers open to the public, and a few even feature a night-time telescope you can look through. Among the best to visit are:
Arecibo Observatory, Puerto Rico.
Kitt Peak National Observatory, Tucson, Arizona.
McDonald Observatory, Fort Davis, Texas.
Mount Palomar Observatory, Pasadena, California.
Mount Wilson Observatory, Los Angeles, California.
The Very Large Array, Socorro, New Mexico.

Nearly all the observatories and planetariums have bookshops where you can buy anything from a bumper sticker to an expensive telescope.

Index